TWIST!

Philippa Bateman

RISING STARS

Tasha was on her laptop.

JJ, look at this! There's a hip-hop gig at the sports stand.

"I can't dance!" said JJ.

"I'll download some hip-hop steps," said Tasha.
Hip-Hop dance steps

"JJ, stand up! I'll call out the steps. Stamp, twist, stamp, twist," said Tasha.

"Stamp, stamp, twist ..." said JJ.

"No, JJ! Think! Don't twist when you have to stamp," said Tasha.

“Then don’t say it so fast!” said JJ.

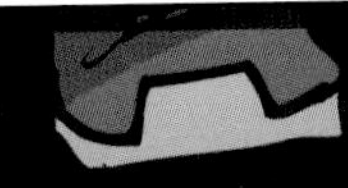

"Feel the beat," said Tasha.

"I feel like a drink," said JJ.

Stamp, stamp, twist, stamp ... ow!
"What is it?" asked Tasha.

"I think I've got cramp! You do it.
I'll call the steps," yelled JJ.

Trust me. This is not for us!
HIP-HOP
Win £50
CLOSED

How come?

The gig was last week!
I know!